A Leader's Guide to
I'm Like You, You're Like Me

A Child's Book About Understanding and Celebrating Each Other

By
Cindy Gainer

Copyright © 1998 by Cindy Gainer

All rights reserved under International and Pan-American Copyright Conventions. Unless otherwise noted, no part of this book may be reproduced, stored in a retrieval system, or transmitted in any form or by any means, electronic, mechanical, photocopying, recording or otherwise, without express written permission of the publisher, except for brief quotations or critical reviews.

> At the time of this book's publication, all facts and figures cited are the most current available; all telephone numbers, addresses, and Web site URLs are accurate and active; all publications, organizations, Web sites, and other resources exist as described in this book; and all have been verified. The author and Free Spirit Publishing make no warranty or guarantee concerning the information and materials given out by organizations or content found at Web sites, and we are not responsible for any changes that occur after this book's publication. If you find an error or believe that a resource listed here is not as described, please contact Free Spirit Publishing. Parents, teachers, and other adults: We strongly urge you to monitor children's use of the Internet.

Some of the information in the Notes on page 2 and page 57 and all of "What to Do If You Suspect That a Child Is Being Abused" on page 59 are adapted from A Leader's Guide to We Can Get Along: A Child's Book of Choices by Lauren Murphy Payne and Claudia Rohling (Minneapolis: Free Spirit Publishing, 1997). Used by permission.

Edited by Marjorie Lisovskis
Author photograph by William C. Matrisch

10 9 8 7 6 5 4
Printed in the United States of America

Free Spirit Publishing Inc.
217 Fifth Avenue North, Suite 200
Minneapolis, MN 55401-1299
(612) 338-2068
help4kids@freespirit.com
www.freespirit.com

The following are registered trademarks of Free Spirit Publishing Inc.:

FREE SPIRIT®
FREE SPIRIT PUBLISHING®
SELF-HELP FOR TEENS®
SELF-HELP FOR KIDS®
WORKS FOR KIDS®
THE FREE SPIRITED CLASSROOM®

DEDICATION

To Bill and August, who share my life.
It is my blessing to share in theirs.

And to William A. Sorrels, M.Ed.,
for his invaluable knowledge and encouragement.

Contents

Introduction 1

Comparing
Lesson One: I'm Like Others 5
Lesson Two: I'm Unique 9
Lesson Three: I'd Like to Get to Know You 13
Lesson Four: Our Bodies Are Different 16
Lesson Five: We All Started Out the Same 20
Lesson Six: I Can Do Things by Myself 23
Lesson Seven: We Have Different Families 26
Lesson Eight: We Celebrate Special Days 30

Acceptance
Lesson Nine: We Can Share and Trust Each Other 33
Lesson Ten: We Can Be Friends 36

Listening
Lesson Eleven: Tell Me Something About You 40
Lesson Twelve: We Have Stories to Tell 43

Understanding
Lesson Thirteen: We Like Different Things 45
Lesson Fourteen: I Can Tell You What I'm Feeling 48
Lesson Fifteen: I Like to Be Understood 51

Kindness
Lesson Sixteen: I Can Be Kind 55
Lesson Seventeen: I Can Help 60

Cooperation
Lesson Eighteen: I Can Be Patient 64
Lesson Nineteen: We Can Work Together 67

Putting It All Together
Lesson Twenty: We Can Cooperate and Have Fun Together 70

Recommended Readings and Resources 72

About the Author/Illustrator 73

List of Reproducible Pages

Letters to Parents/Caregivers 3–4

Leaf Pattern 8

10 Ways Children Are Alike and Different 12

10 Healthy Things I Can Do for My Body 19

Family Figures 29

10 Phrases That Help Children Share 35

Buddy Shapes 38

5 Ways to Listen 42

10 Ways to Say "I'm Sorry" 54

30 Kind Things to Say 58

20 Ways Children Can Help at Home 63

Introduction

Children need to feel accepted, valued, and understood so they can learn to accept, value, and understand others. The early childhood classroom (or day care center, or wherever young children happen to be) is the ideal place to introduce children to these concepts. In places like this, children begin to:

- interact with people who are different from themselves
- share, take turns, and work and play together
- discover and develop unique traits and skills
- explore the many ways they're like and unlike others.

This leader's guide is a companion to the children's book, *I'm Like You, You're Like Me: A Child's Book About Understanding and Celebrating Each Other*. The activities in this guide, together with the children's book, introduce tolerance. Through the lessons, children explore six concepts:

- comparing
- acceptance
- listening
- understanding
- kindness
- cooperation.

The children's book presents these overlapping ideas through vibrant illustrations and gentle prose. Because children have different interests, learning styles, and abilities, the lessons in this guide let you and your group of children explore the ideas through curriculum-related activities, including art, literature, math, science, health, social studies, dramatic play, music, movement, and cooking.

HOW TO USE THIS BOOK

A Leader's Guide to I'm Like You, You're Like Me is designed to be used with children in preschool, kindergarten, elementary school, day care, religious school, youth groups, counseling groups, homes, and other settings. Through reading, listening, thinking, talking, sharing, creating, and working together, children learn that they have common interests and abilities as well as individual characteristics.

Before beginning the lessons, you'll want to read the children's book and look at the illustrations. Think about what the words and pictures mean to you. You can draw on your own feelings and ideas when you discuss the book with the children.

On page 3, you'll find a letter to parents and caregivers introducing the "I'm Like You, You're Like Me" program. If you're teaching the lessons in a school or group setting, you may want to photocopy this letter to send home with the children in your group.

On page 4, you'll find a second letter you may want to complete and use when sending program materials home with the children.

The children's book is divided into 20 two-page sections that correspond to the 20 lessons in the leader's guide. Each lesson has these parts:

- the lesson theme, described by the title of the lesson
- an opening statement about the theme and the concept being presented
- the lesson concept and a list of learning goals

- guidelines for reading and teaching the ideas in the children's book, along with suggested discussion questions

- activities to do with the children

- suggested follow-up activities to reinforce the ideas taught in the lesson.

Some lessons also include a Home Handout for you to photocopy, if you wish, and send home with the children. These handouts share some of the ideas the children are exploring without requiring families to do any tasks at home.

The children's book presents ideas in a sequence. You'll find the lessons most effective when taught in this sequence. The concepts of comparing, acceptance, listening, understanding, kindness, and cooperation are first introduced and explored individually. Later, they are integrated to provide children with a broader understanding of what it means to accept and value others.

The individual activities are designed to be flexible. You may expand them or adapt them to fit your particular group. Do whatever works best with the children in your care, depending on their interests and attention spans.

Use these suggestions to help children gain the most from the activities in "I'm Like You, You're Like Me":

- Be open to children's interpretations of concepts. A child may see a relationship that's a mystery to you, but has great meaning for the child. Ask questions that invite the child to explain what he or she is thinking. Of course, don't push a child to speak or elaborate if the child doesn't wish to do so. If a child's remark seems inconsistent with the lesson, acknowledge it and look for a way to tie it to the concept being discussed. For example, during a discussion of ways to show kindness, a child might say, "I like to watch TV." You could reply, "Alex says he likes TV. What are some ways people on TV show kindness to each other?"

- Be patient with the time it takes children to respond or to complete tasks. Some children may find an activity overwhelming. For example, a child may have difficulty drawing a picture of herself at a carnival. You might suggest that the child draw the horse she would choose on the merry-go-round, the cotton candy she would eat, or the animal she would pet at the barn.

- Display the work of every child. Allow children to take their work home, if they wish.

- Model understanding and acceptance. As teachers, we are always modeling words and actions. This is especially true when teaching tolerance and empathy. Also make it a point to notice and remark on children's positive words and actions: "I noticed the jump-rope group did a good job of taking turns on the playground today." "Thank you for being so friendly and helpful to our visitor."

Finally, have fun in your role as teacher, leader, or caregiver. Being part of children's learning experiences is a joy and a privilege. When children know you're enjoying the lessons, they're more likely to enjoy them, too.

Cindy Gainer

NOTE: "I'm Like You, You're Like Me" is designed to teach children tolerance and respect for others. While discussing these concepts, it is possible that a child in your care may indicate that he or she is being abused in some way. We urge you to read "If You Suspect That a Child Is Being Abused" in Lesson Sixteen on page 59 and act appropriately. If you're teaching this course in a school, preschool, day care, or other group setting, be sure that you know the policies and procedures of your school or organization regarding abuse and the discovery or suspicion of abuse.

Dear Parent/Caregiver,

We will soon be starting an exciting new program called "I'm Like You, You're Like Me." This program is intended to help children learn about and appreciate some of the many ways people are alike and different.

The program has 20 lessons based on the picture book titled *I'm Like You, You're Like Me.* This book uses simple words and colorful pictures to introduce and reinforce concepts like acceptance, understanding, and cooperation. The lessons present activities that help children apply the ideas in the book to their own lives.

From time to time, your child will bring home handouts related to the lessons. These handouts will tell you more about the ideas we're exploring as a group.

We'll begin the lessons on _____ (date). If you have any questions, please feel free to call me.

Sincerely,

_____

Telephone: _____

Dear Parent/Caregiver,

Attached are some materials from "I'm Like You, You're Like Me," which is designed to help children learn about and appreciate the ways people are alike and different. I'm sending you these materials from your child's course because:

If you have any questions about these materials or about "I'm Like You, You're Like Me," please contact me.

Sincerely,

_____

Telephone: _____

LESSON ONE

I'm Like Others

Children need to learn that all people are alike in many ways. Knowing this will help them begin to identify with, understand, and appreciate others and feel more confident and comfortable with other people.

CONCEPT

Comparing

GOALS

1. To explore children's similar qualities and interests.

2. To help children achieve a sense of belonging to a group.

3. To reinforce each child's individual identity within the group.

DISCUSSING THE BOOK

(pages 2 and 3)

You and I are alike in many ways.
We may be the same age
or live on the same street.
We may go to the same school
or even have the same name.

Read the page to the children and show the accompanying illustration. Ask questions like:

- "How are these children alike?"

- "What are some things that all these children might like to do?"

- "What are other ways that these children might be alike?"

- "How are these children like you? How are they like other children?"

Encourage the children to notice or imagine as many similarities as possible. If the children point out differences, you might say, "Yes, two are boys and two are girls. How are these girls and boys alike?"

Guide the children to explore beyond physical similarities. For example, if a child says, "All people have two legs," you might respond, "Yes, most people have two legs. What are some other ways people can be alike?" Help the children identify and appreciate the many similarities that bond people together.

ACTIVITY 1
Favorite Toy Cut-outs

Materials needed:

- Magazines or catalogs featuring photographs of nonviolent toys
- Safety scissors
- Construction paper
- White glue
- Glitter or fabric trim

Tell the children that they can make posters showing their favorite toys. Have the children cut out pictures of favorite toys (which could be toys they have or toys they'd like) and glue them onto construction paper. They can decorate their posters with glitter or fabric trim, if they wish.

While the children work, call attention to the fact that they all enjoy toys. You might say, "I see that both Brett and LaShonda have cut out Mr. Potato Head," or, "It looks like lots of children like LEGOs."

Display the posters and invite the children to talk about their favorite toys. Ask the group:

- "What are some toys that lots of you like?"
- "What's a toy that only one or two people cut out? Who else likes that toy?"
- "Do all children like toys? Why?"

ACTIVITY 2
Group Tree Poster

Materials needed:

- Posterboard or chart paper
- Bare tree branches or brown marker
- Tape
- Copies of the leaf pattern on page 8
- Safety scissors
- Crayons, colored pencils, and/or washable markers

Optional:

- Additional posterboard
- Scissors (for you)
- Construction paper (any colors)

Ahead of time, make a tree by taping branches on posterboard or drawing them on chart paper. Label the poster "Our Colorful Autumn Tree."

Hand out copies of the leaf pattern and invite the children to cut out and decorate a leaf (or leaves) however they choose. Have or help the children write their names on their leaf. Attach the paper leaves to the tree branches.

Admire the tree together. You might ask, "How are the leaves on our tree alike? How are they different?" Remind the children that even though each leaf is different, everyone helped cut out and decorate leaves using similar materials. Conclude by asking the children, "Would our tree be as nice if we hadn't made so many different kinds of leaves for it?"

Optional: If you wish, make leaf tracing shapes by tracing the pattern onto posterboard and cutting it out. Have children trace the pattern onto colored construction paper. Older children may enjoy drawing their own leaf shapes.

FOLLOW-UP

1. From time to time, ask the children to name ways they are similar to others.

2. Have the children form pairs and talk about their similarities. Encourage the children to think of a variety of similarities, including those that are emotional (for example, shared excitement about riding a roller coaster) and those that are social (for example, a common interest in collecting dolls or rocks).

3. Point out similarities you notice in your classroom. You might say, "I see most of you are excited about all the snow that fell last night. What will you do in the snow today? Who else wants to do that?"

4. Extend Activity 2 by exploring the scientific similarities among leaves. Compare leaves from the same tree species and those from different species. Investigate why most leaves are green in spring and summer, then change color in the fall.

LESSON ONE HANDOUT: LEAF PATTERN

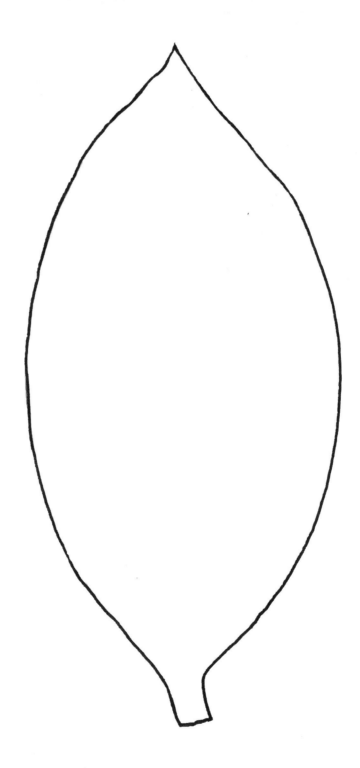

LESSON TWO
I'm Unique

> Recognizing and appreciating similarities and differences helps children develop positive relationships with others. At the same time, it builds a sense of pride and self-confidence.

CONCEPT

Comparing

GOALS

1. To explore children's individual qualities and interests.
2. To help children understand that differences are something to appreciate.
3. To support children in feeling good about themselves and their unique qualities and abilities.
4. To reinforce children's appreciation of how they're like others.

DISCUSSING THE BOOK

(pages 4 and 5)

We are different from each other, too.
Our hair may be brown or blond or red or black.
Our eyes may be blue or brown or green.
Our skin may be dark or light or in between.

Read the page to the children and show the accompanying illustration. Ask questions like:

- "How are these children different from each other?"
- "What do you think is something that *this* child likes to do?" (Point to one child.)
- "What do you think is something different that *this* child likes to do?" (Point to a different child.)

9

- "What are some ways you might be different from one of these children?"
- "How can children be different and still be friends? How can a child who likes to do *one* thing be friends with a child who likes to do another thing?"

Some children will probably notice many physical differences. Encourage the children to imagine other differences as well—for example, in interests, abilities, and feelings.

Help the children understand why differences are valuable. You might ask, "Why is it nice to be different in some ways? What would happen if you and your friend are exactly alike? How could your families tell you apart? What would it be like if everybody loved to play T-ball but nobody liked to jump rope?"

ACTIVITY 1
Fingerprint Pictures
Materials needed:

- Stamp pad with washable ink
- Large sheets of drawing paper
- Magnifying glasses
- Crayons, colored pencils, and/or washable markers

Have the children look at their hands and fingers. Ask the group how their hands are alike and different.

Tell the children that they can compare fingerprints. Demonstrate by pressing your finger into the stamp pad until it has plenty of ink on it, then pressing it firmly on the paper. Allow time for each child to make at least one fingerprint.

Let groups of three or four children use a magnifying glass to compare fingerprints and discuss how the prints are different.

Then give the children drawing materials and invite them to create pictures from their fingerprints. The children can use the stamp pad to make additional fingerprints, if they wish.

Circulate among the children as they work, and comment on the uniqueness of their fingerprints and drawings: "I see that Chloe has made a fingerprint caterpillar, and Ramón has drawn his family eating dinner. I like all the different things you're making from your fingerprints!"

ACTIVITY 2
Me Mobiles
Materials needed:

- Small white paper plates (several per child)
- Paper punch
- Scissors (for you)
- String, yarn, or brightly colored ribbon
- Crayons, colored pencils, and/or washable markers

Before the activity, punch a hole near the outer edge of each paper plate, and run a piece of yarn or ribbon through the hole.

Talk for a minute with the children about their special traits, interests, and abilities. You might say, "Each of us is unique. We come from our own families. We like to do certain things. I live with my husband, Bill, and my son, August. We like to play hide-and-seek outside on nice days. Here at school, I like to read and do art projects with all of you. You've noticed that I like to sing while I work, too. Those are just some of the special things about me."

Then say, "Think about what's special about you. Who do you live with? What do you like to do together? What are some other things you like to do? Play ball? Ride a bike? What do you like to do at school?"

Tell the children that they can make "Me Mobiles." Ask them to draw a few pictures of things that will tell the group what's special about them. Distribute the paper plates and drawing materials. Circulate among the children and ask them to describe their drawings. You may wish to summarize each child's comments by writing or helping the child write a brief description on the plate with a marker or pencil. Comment on how the children's art demonstrates ways they're alike and different: "Tessa has a cat and a dog. She likes to play in the park with her dog. Yuri has a dog, too, named Velga. His family speaks Russian to Velga."

Tie each child's completed drawings to a long piece of string or yarn. Display the "Me Mobiles" on the blackboard, ceiling, or windows.

FOLLOW-UP

1. Invite volunteers to explain their "Me Mobiles." Encourage the children to notice the ways the mobiles show that they're alike and different. Point out that although many children have things in common, each mobile shows a combination of things that make each child unique.

2. Remind the children that being different isn't bad. Encourage them to describe differences without using the words "good" or "bad." If a child says, "I'm a good girl because I know how to read," you might respond, "You really like to read." Reinforce the children's strengths by encouraging them to share their strengths with others. For example, if a child has difficulty tying his shoes, enlist a child who can tie shoes to help him.

3. Copy the Home Handout for this lesson, "10 Ways Children Are Alike and Different," to send home to the children's families. You might use the letter on page 4 to introduce the handout. Encourage the children to tell their families what they're learning about being alike and different.

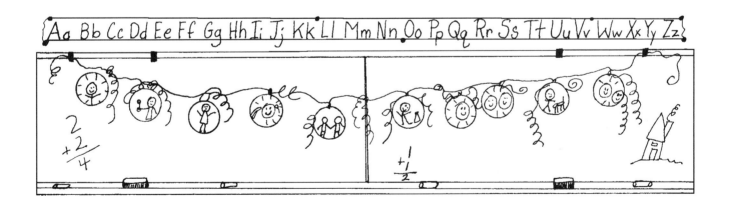

Lesson Two 11

LESSON TWO HOME HANDOUT

10 WAYS CHILDREN ARE ALIKE AND DIFFERENT

1. *Children have families and important people in their lives.* One family is big. Another is small. Another is in between. Each child's family is unique.

2. *Children like to play outdoors.* One child likes T-ball. Another likes to swim. Another likes to swing and swing and swing.

3. *Children like books.* One child wants to read the story to you. Another wants you to read the story aloud. Another wants to do it both ways.

4. *Children like to help.* One child likes to help cook supper. Another likes to help care for pets. Another likes to feed a baby brother or sister.

5. *Children like to laugh.* One child likes knock-knock jokes. Another likes tongue twisters. Another likes to play jokes on *you*.

6. *Children like to learn about nature.* One child likes to plant flowers and collect leaves. Another likes to find rocks. Another likes to watch the stars.

7. *Children need to eat.* One child likes oatmeal. Another likes oatmeal cookies. Another doesn't like oatmeal at all!

8. *Children like to move.* One child likes to run. Another likes to dance. Another likes to jump rope.

9. *Children like to make believe.* One child is a scary pirate. Another is the queen of the forest. Another is a daddy who sings his baby to sleep.

10. *Children have feelings.* One child feels happy. Another feels sad. Children need to know they're loved no matter what they're feeling.

From *A Leader's Guide to I'm Like You, You're Like Me,* by Cindy Gainer, copyright © 1998 Free Spirit Publishing Inc., Minneapolis, MN; 800/735-7323 *(www.freespirit.com).* This page may be photocopied for individual, classroom, or group work only.

LESSON THREE

I'd Like to Get to Know You

> By providing opportunities for children to get to know each other, we create situations in which they can begin to appreciate their similarities and discover their differences.

CONCEPT

Comparing

GOALS

1. To provide an opportunity for children to get to know one another.
2. To reinforce children's appreciation of similarities and differences.

DISCUSSING THE BOOK

(pages 6 and 7)

It's fun to find ways I'm like you and you're like me.
It's fun to find ways we're different.
One of us is bigger, and the other is smaller.
One of us has curly hair,
the other has straight hair.

Read the page to the children and show the accompanying illustration. Ask questions like:

- "What are these children doing?"
- "What do you think they might be thinking?"
- "What are some ways you and your friends are alike and different?"

- "Why do you think these children like to play dress-up?"
- "What are some things you like to do with your friends?"
- "How can children find out what their friends like to do?"

Point out that *comparing* is one way friends learn about how they're alike and different. Emphasize that children can get to know each other better while they talk and play.

ACTIVITY
"I'd Like to Get to Know You" Hopscotch

Materials needed:

- Colored chalk or washable markers
- Sidewalk or pavement, or heavy paper and masking tape
- Small beanbags

Prepare for this activity by drawing hopscotch patterns on the pavement or on heavy paper taped to the floor. Create one hopscotch pattern for every three or four children. Write the numbers 1–10 inside the squares (see pattern).

Tell the children that they can play "I'd Like to Get to Know You" Hopscotch. Explain that they can decorate the squares in ways that tell the others about them. For example, the children might:

- draw their own picture
- write their name
- create a design using their favorite color
- draw a picture of something they like to do.

Allow several minutes for the children to decorate the hopscotch squares. Circulate among the children and comment on what you see in their drawings: "I see that Marco likes the color purple. Both Benjie and Mary have drawn pictures of their baby brothers. Shauna has made an interesting design."

After everyone has finished, gather the group together and ask for volunteers to describe the drawings. Emphasize what the children are learning about each other. Remind them that they're alike in many ways and unique in many ways.

Explain the game, which is slightly different from traditional hopscotch: Children stand at the bottom, in front of square 1. Each child in turn tosses a beanbag and hops to the end of the board, being careful not to hop on the square where the beanbag landed. Then the child hops back, picking up the beanbag (but not hopping on its square) on the way back to square 1.

FOLLOW-UP

1. Have the children pair up and ask three questions to learn more about their partner. Suggest that they ask about their partner's family, hobbies, or favorite book or sport. Then invite volunteers to tell the group what they've learned about their partner.

2. Have the children play a game called "Mirror Mimic." Begin by saying, "We're going to play a game called 'Mirror Mimic.' What do you think that means?" Once the children understand the idea behind the activity, explain the game: The children will play in pairs. One child will be the leader and the other will follow. (Assure the children that everyone will get a turn to both lead and follow.) The two children stand facing each other, as if looking into a mirror. The leader moves and the follower tries to match the movements exactly. After everyone has played, ask the children what they noticed about their partners.

LESSON FOUR

Our Bodies Are Different

> Body awareness provides a concrete sense of identity. Children's awareness of size, shape, and ability affects how they perceive themselves and others. It's important for children to accept and appreciate their bodies. Adults can support this by reinforcing positive body concepts for every child.

CONCEPT

Comparing

GOALS

1. To help children recognize and appreciate their own unique physical characteristics and abilities.

2. To encourage children to accept and appreciate the physical characteristics and abilities of others.

3. To emphasize the importance of caring for your body.

DISCUSSING THE BOOK

(pages 8 and 9)

I like my body and how I look.
My body is just right for me.
Your body is just right for you, too.

Read the page to the children and show the accompanying illustration. Ask questions like:

- "How are these children's bodies alike?"

- "How are they different?"

- "What do these children's bodies help the children do?"

- "What are some things your body can help you do?"

Emphasize that although physical differences make people unique, each person's body is just right for that person.

ACTIVITY 1
All the Beautiful Fish

Materials needed:

- Books and magazines depicting a variety of fish
- Large sheets of drawing paper
- Tempera paints and brushes

Show the children some of the books and magazines depicting fish. Discuss how different the fish are. You might say: "Look at this fish. How would you describe its body? Now look at this other fish. How are these fish different? Why do you think one fish is so big and the other is so small?" Help the children appreciate how each fish's body helps it. For example, a fish's color might help it blend into its surroundings. Its fins and tail help it move through the water.

Tell the children that they can paint pictures of different fish. For younger children, demonstrate a way to paint a simple fish using an oval for the body and a triangle for a tail. Give the children paper and paints to create their fish. Encourage them to make their fish either real looking or make-believe. Comment on the array of colors and shapes that make each fish unique. Display the fish pictures on the walls or bulletin board.

Optional: Use tempera paints to create a background mural of ocean water and seaweed. You may wish to include other sea creatures such as starfish or sand dollars. Display the children's fish so they appear to swim in the ocean.

ACTIVITY 2
Class Height Chart

Materials needed:

- White paper strips, approximately 9" x 2"
- Washable markers
- Crepe-paper streamers
- Masking tape
- Safety scissors

Optional:

- Yardsticks or tape measures

Have the children write their names on the white paper strips. Then have the children work in pairs. Give each pair crepe paper and scissors and explain that one partner will measure the other partner. One partner will stand against the wall, while the other unrolls the paper until it's the same length as the child, then cuts it. (Older children can use a yardstick or tape measure to measure the length of their streamers.) The children then tape their own crepe-paper lengths to the paper with their name on it, with the name strip at the bottom.

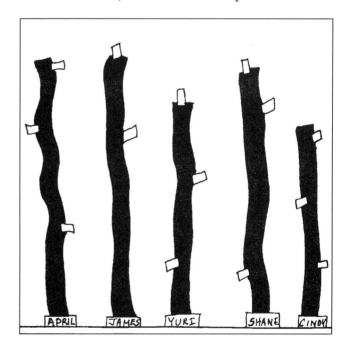

Lesson Four

Hang the lengths along a wall, with the name strips touching the floor. Label the display "Here's How Tall We Are."

Remind the children, "Some people are tall. Some are small. Your height is just right for you."

FOLLOW-UP

1. As a follow-up to Activity 1, read *Swimmy* by Leo Lionni (see "Recommended Readings and Resources," page 72). Talk about how Swimmy's color allowed him to help the other fish and what Swimmy learned about being different.

2. As a follow-up to Activity 2, have or help the children add crepe paper to their strips to show how they continue to grow.

3. Have children write or dictate sentences describing what their bodies can do. Encourage children to avoid words that judge, such as "good at," "pretty," or "fat." Offer examples: "My legs are strong. I can kick a ball a long way." "My long fingers help me play the piano." If you like, assemble the sentences into a class book with the title "Our Bodies Can Do Many Things."

4. Invite the children to make handprint pictures by dipping their hands into tempera paint or fingerpaint and then pressing them on paper. When the paint has dried, children can outline the handprints with glue and sprinkle glitter over the wet glue. Compare the sizes, shapes, and prints of the children's hands.

5. Using the Home Handout for this lesson, "10 Healthy Things I Can Do for My Body," talk with children about ways to keep their bodies healthy. Send the handout home to their families. You might use the letter on page 4 to introduce the handout. Encourage the children to tell their families what they're learning about the ways their bodies are just right for them.

LESSON FOUR HOME HANDOUT

10 HEALTHY THINGS I CAN DO FOR MY BODY

I can:

1. Eat when I feel hungry.

2. Drink lots of water, fruit juice, and milk.

3. Rest or sleep when I feel tired.

4. Wash and dry my hands and body.

5. Brush my teeth.

6. Brush or comb my hair.

7. Cover my nose and mouth when I cough or sneeze.

8. Exercise my body to help keep it strong.

9. Tell someone when I don't feel well.

10. Be glad that I have a body that's just right for me.

From *A Leader's Guide to I'm Like You, You're Like Me,* by Cindy Gainer, copyright © 1998 Free Spirit Publishing Inc., Minneapolis, MN; 800/735-7323 *(www.freespirit.com).* This page may be photocopied for individual, classroom, or group work only.

LESSON FIVE

We All Started Out the Same

Children often enjoy learning and talking about what they were like as babies. Because everyone was once an infant, sharing information about babyhood can help children develop a sense of kinship and discover and explore other similarities. This also reinforces the universal experience of growth and change.

CONCEPT

Comparing

GOALS

1. To help children recognize the shared history of babyhood.

2. To foster children's understanding that they will continue to change and grow.

DISCUSSING THE BOOK

(pages 11 and 12)

I was a baby once, and so were you.
It's fun to look at our baby pictures.
See how little we used to be!

Read the page to the children and show the accompanying illustration. Ask questions like:

- "What are these children doing? How can you tell?"

- "Were the children in the picture ever babies? How do you know?"

- "Who do you know who was *never* a baby?"

- "What things do you see here that babies need? How do babies use these things?"
- "What are some things you can do now that you couldn't do when you were a baby?"

Children who are adopted or who live in foster families may not have heard stories about when they were babies. To set an inviting tone for all children, say something like, "We were all babies once. We all ate and slept and cried. We all wanted to be hugged. We all have learned to do many things since we were babies."

ACTIVITY 1
Class Baby Book

Materials needed:

- Pictures of babies from catalogs, magazines, and newspapers
- Safety scissors
- Sheets of 12" x 18" construction paper
- White glue
- Washable markers and/or pencils
- 12" x 18" posterboard for the book's cover
- Hole punch and yarn or metal rings to fasten the book

Ask the children, "What are some things babies do?" Some answers might include crying, eating, sleeping, and slobbering. Remind children that they were all babies once—and that you were, too!

Explain to the children that they will be making pages for a book about babies. Help the children plan their pages. If they need ideas, suggest one of the following:

- Make a collage of pictures of babies doing all kinds of things.
- Show pictures of babies doing one thing, such as eating or sleeping.
- Show pictures of things babies need, such as diapers, baby food, and bottles.
- Write a sentence or a story about a baby.

Have or help the children cut out pictures of babies and glue the pictures to the construction paper. If they wish, the children can decorate or write on their pages with markers. You may choose to summarize each child's comments by writing or helping the child write a brief description on the page with a marker or pencil. Before collecting the children's work, have them write their name on their pages.

Assemble the pages into a class book entitled "We All Started Out as Babies."

ACTIVITY 2
Living Things Grow and Change

Materials needed:

- Clean, empty plastic yogurt containers (8 oz.)
- Crayons, colored pencils, and/or washable markers
- White or colored paper
- Scissors and tape (for you)
- Potting soil
- Small potatoes with lots of eyes
- Watering can
- Plastic ice-cream buckets (1 gallon) or outdoor growing space

Beforehand, cut strips of white or colored paper to fit around the outside of each yogurt container.

Lesson Five

Introduce the activity by talking about growth and change. You might say, "We've talked about how people grow and change. Many things in nature grow and change, too. Who can tell me about something that changes in nature?" Encourage the children to suggest a variety of natural changes.

Then say, "Today we're going to plant potatoes. Then we'll be able to watch our potatoes grow and change."

The children can work individually or in pairs. Begin by having them write their names on the bottom of their yogurt container. Then show the children how the paper strip fits around each container. Allow time for the children to decorate their container covers, then have or help them tape the covers in place.

Help the children fill the containers with a small amount of potting soil, place the potatoes on top, and cover them with soil. Place the potato plants on a windowsill and water them. Have the children continue to water their plants as needed, and watch the potatoes begin to grow.

Once the foliage is about two to three inches high, transplant the potatoes into gallon ice-cream buckets or an outdoor garden. Place indoor plants in a sunny window or under strong artificial light. Water the plants as needed. When the foliage turns brown, the potatoes will be ready to harvest.

Follow-Up

1. For older children, a variation on the class baby book is to create a book that shows what older children—"big kids"—can do. Older children may also enjoy reminiscing about a time when they were "little." Ask the children how they're different now from when they were "little."

2. The children may enjoy moving like babies. Have them lie and kick their legs in the air, crawl in a circle, and "toddle" a short distance.

3. Talk about ways the children have learned to move since they were babies. Have the children walk, jump, and run in place.

LESSON SIX

I Can Do Things by Myself

Children need to feel in control. One way they can achieve this is by doing things on their own. Practicing independent activities is important for children; equally important is helping children identify the skills they've mastered.

CONCEPT

Comparing

GOALS

1. To provide an opportunity for children to carry out an independent activity.

2. To provide a forum for children to share their abilities with others.

DISCUSSING THE BOOK

(pages 12 and 13)

I've learned how to do some things by myself, and so have you.
We can both tie our shoes.
We can both ride a bike.
We can both write our names.

Read the page to the children and show the accompanying illustration. Ask questions like:

- "What are these children doing?"

- "Do you think all these children have the same skill in riding a bike? Why or why not?"

- "What do you think are some other things these children can do by themselves?"
- "What things can you do by yourself?"

ACTIVITY 1
"All by Myself" Munchies

Materials needed:

- Purchased fruit that the children can prepare with little or no assistance (such as oranges, seedless grapes, and bananas)
- Strainer for washing the fruit
- Dish towels
- Butter knives
- Large plate(s) for serving the fruit
- Party toothpicks
- Napkins
- Dish detergent

Tell the children that they're going to do something by themselves: prepare a snack for the group. After they've washed their hands carefully, ask them to select a piece of fruit to prepare. Have them wash the fruit and pat it dry.

Then give the children butter knives and tell them to peel, section, and/or cut the fruit into bite-sized pieces. Help the children only as much as needed. Don't worry if the fruit gets squashed or if the sizes of the segments vary widely.

Show the children how to insert a toothpick into each fruit piece and place it on the serving plate.

Once the plates are full of fruit, share and enjoy the snack. As you eat, point out that the children were able to prepare this snack all by themselves. Talk together about other things the children can do by themselves. If someone mentions something that not everyone can do yet, point out that each person grows and learns at a different rate. Emphasize that everyone is able to do some things by themselves and contribute to the group.

After eating, ask for volunteers to wash the serving plates and clean the eating area.

ACTIVITY 2
"I Can" Cards

Materials needed:

- 4" x 6" file cards
- Crayons, colored pencils, and/or washable markers
- Decorative materials such as stickers, glitter, ribbon, or fabric
- White glue

Say to the children, "You've been thinking about things you can do by yourself. What are some of the things we've talked about?" Briefly review some of the things the children can do on their own.

Then invite the children to make greeting cards that show something they can do now that they couldn't always do. You might say, "Show me what you can draw now that you couldn't draw when you were a baby. Or draw something you can do now that you couldn't always do." Show them the materials they can use to decorate their cards. Suggest that they give their "I Can" card to a family member or friend.

As the children work, circulate among them and comment on what different children are depicting on their cards. "I see that Tu Yen knows how to make his bed." "Lisa knows how to draw a spaceship now." "Aparna can feed her baby sister her supper." As needed, write or help the children write a description of the pictures they've drawn on their cards.

FOLLOW-UP

1. Periodically at the end of the day, ask the children to name something they did by themselves during the day. Make a point of noticing and remarking on what the children are doing on their own: writing, cleaning up after an activity, working on the computer, or helping someone.

2. Use a Polaroid camera to take pictures of the children doing things on their own. Post the pictures on the bulletin board. Talk about how the board is filling up with activities the children can do by themselves.

LESSON SEVEN

We Have Different Families

There are many kinds of families: Large families and small families. Dual-parent and single-parent families. Stepfamilies, blended families, and extended families. Traditional and nontraditional families. Families where siblings are close in age and families where they're not. Sharing these details broadens children's understanding of the definition of *family*. While learning about different families, children also begin to identify the qualities families have in common.

CONCEPT

Comparing

GOALS

1. To help the children recognize that there are a variety of family compositions and settings.

2. To provide a chance for the children to appreciate and take pride in their families.

3. To introduce the children to the ways that families are alike and different.

DISCUSSING THE BOOK

(pages 14 and 15)

We have different families.
Some families have many people.
Some families have few people.

Read the page to the children and show the accompanying illustration. Ask questions like:

- "Who do you think these people are?"
- "Why do you think that?"
- "How is your family like this family?"

- "How is your family different from this family?"
- "What does it mean to be a family?"

> **NOTE:** Your group probably includes children from diverse family situations. All families experience stress at different times and in different ways. You'll want to be especially alert and sensitive in your responses during this discussion. It's important that all children learn to accept and respect the differences among families.

ACTIVITY 1
"My Family Place" Diorama

Materials needed:

- Copies of the family figures handout on page 29 (several handouts per child)
- Scissors (for you)
- Shoe boxes
- White glue
- Crayons, colored pencils, and/or washable markers
- Safety scissors

Optional:

- Nontoxic acrylic paints and brushes

> **NOTE:** Children have a variety of places that they call home. For some children, that place may be a temporary one, such as a shelter. It's possible that a child may feel ashamed about living in a shelter. In this case, use your knowledge of the child along with your own judgment and discretion. If you like, you can adapt the activity to focus strictly on *family* rather than *family place* by having children mount images of family members on large paper plates.

- Precut squares of construction paper for windows and doors

Before conducting the activity, cut out at least one family figure to use when explaining the activity to the children. (You may want to cut out all of the family figures.) Because of their simple shape, many children will be able to cut them out on their own.

Tell the children that they can use a shoe box to make a "family place." Explain that they can illustrate their real family or a make-believe one by cutting, drawing, and coloring pictures of family members and gluing them into the box. Show the children how to fold a figure on the dotted line and glue it to the box bottom.

As the children work on their family place, circulate and assist them as needed in planning, cutting, and gluing. Encourage the children to include pets as part of their family group. Comment on the different people and pets you're seeing. You might say, "The different families I'm seeing are really interesting!"

Lesson Seven 27

Optional: If you wish, have the children paint and/or decorate their shoe-box homes before they create their dioramas. Give the boxes plenty of time to dry before using them.

ACTIVITY 2
Family Picture Frame

Materials needed:

- Sheets of 8½" x 10" tagboard
- Unlined file cards (3½" x 5" or 4" x 6")
- White glue
- Crayons, colored pencils, and/or washable markers
- Art supplies such as buttons, costume jewels, feathers, beads, colored toothpicks, glitter, confetti, yarn, ribbon, wrapping paper, pipe cleaners

Tell the children they can make a picture frame for a drawing or photograph of their family or themselves.

Show the children how to glue the file card to the middle of the tagboard. Explain that this is where the picture will go. Then allow time for the children to decorate the frames however they like.

When they're finished, tell the children they can draw a picture to go in the frame or bring a photograph from home. Display the pictures under the heading "We Have Many Different Families."

FOLLOW-UP

1. As a follow-up to Activity 1, read the book *Houses and Homes* by Ann Morris (see "Recommended Readings and Resources," page 72). Talk about the many different kinds of homes people have all over the world, and about the different families who live in them.

2. Invite the children to tell about a family member or share a family story. You might compile a tape-recording or class book of the children's stories and make it available in the library area.

28   *A Leader's Guide to I'm Like You, You're Like Me*

LESSON SEVEN HANDOUT: FAMILY FIGURES

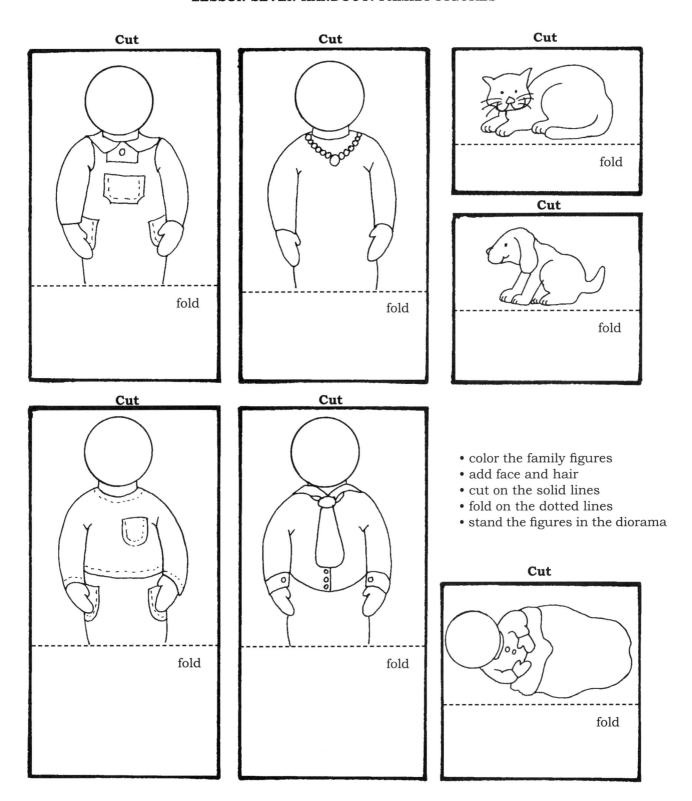

- color the family figures
- add face and hair
- cut on the solid lines
- fold on the dotted lines
- stand the figures in the diorama

LESSON EIGHT

We Celebrate Special Days

A holiday is a celebration of our identity. Activities centered on celebrations and traditions offer children another way to understand how people are similar and different.

CONCEPT

Comparing

GOALS

1. To provide an opportunity for the children to appreciate and take pride in their own celebrations and traditions.

2. To introduce children to unfamiliar occasions and ways of celebrating them.

3. To help children appreciate and respect the different ways in which people celebrate.

DISCUSSING THE BOOK

(pages 16 and 17)

*We celebrate holidays and special days.
Sometimes we celebrate the same holidays.
Sometimes we celebrate different holidays.
Sometimes we celebrate the same holidays
in different ways.*

Read the page to the children and show the accompanying illustration. Ask questions like:

- "What are these children doing?"

- "Why do you think there's a parade?"

- "Why do we have parades?"

NOTE: Some families may not want their child to celebrate any occasions. If this is the case for a child in your classroom, it's a good idea to change your emphasis on *celebrations* to a focus on *traditions*.

Discuss celebrations and traditions. Your questions and comments will vary, depending on your focus for the lesson.

Celebrations:

Say, "A celebration is a way people enjoy special times."

Ask questions like:

- "What could the children in the picture be celebrating?"
- "What does *celebrate* mean?"
- "What are some things our group celebrates?"
- "What are some ways you and your family celebrate special times?"

Traditions:

Say, "A parade that happens every year is a kind of *tradition*. A tradition is something people do again and again."

Ask questions like:

- "What are some traditions we have in our classroom?"
- "What are some traditions you have in your family?"

Some of the group's traditions might include the "Pledge of Allegiance," daily storytime, or a special game played once a week. Some family traditions might include bedtime stories, a special weekly meal, or attending religious services.

ACTIVITY
Celebrations/Traditions Banner

Materials needed:

- Scissors (for you)
- Large pieces of paper (all the same size)
- Crayons, colored pencils, and/or markers
- Tape
- Safety scissors

Tell the children that they can draw pictures for a banner showing lots of different celebrations or traditions. Briefly review what *celebrations* or *traditions* are, and invite or suggest ideas of things the children might draw. The following are a few suggestions for each.

Celebrations:

- Birthday (cake and candles)
- Valentine's Day (cards)
- Fourth of July (fireworks)
- Halloween (costumes)
- Thanksgiving (turkey)
- Christmas (tree)
- Hanukkah (menorah)
- Kwanzaa (candles)
- New Year (noisemakers)
- Chinese New Year (animal dances)

Traditions:

- library day
- field trips

Lesson Eight

- weekly errands
- family reunions
- community festivals

Invite the children to draw their pictures on the large pieces of paper. As the children work, comment on the pictures you're seeing and how they're similar and different. "Kendra's family eats pizza on Friday nights. Jake goes to his dad's for Sunday dinner. Lots of families have food traditions."

When the drawings are finished, tape them together to form a banner. Hang the banner on the wall, down a hallway, or along a blackboard.

FOLLOW-UP

1. Discuss family traditions and celebrations. You might want to bring a traditional object your own family uses, such as a menorah, a colored egg, or a bedtime storybook. Invite the children to tell the group about a family celebration or tradition.

2. Start a class birthday tradition by reading a book about birthdays such as *Happy Birthday!* by Gail Gibbons (see "Recommended Readings and Resources," page 72) on each child's birthday.

LESSON NINE

We Can Share and Trust Each Other

Sharing and taking turns helps children build trust and learn to accept others. Gradually, children will understand that when they share a belonging with someone, the other person won't intentionally lose or damage it. At the same time, children need to recognize that even when people mean well, they can make mistakes. Young children can begin to comprehend this while beginning to build relationships based on trust and acceptance.

CONCEPT

Acceptance

GOALS

1. To provide an opportunity for children to safely share and explore each other's belongings.
2. To address the idea that trusted people can have accidents when using other people's belongings.

DISCUSSING THE BOOK

(pages 18 and 19)

*Even though we're different in some ways, we can enjoy being together.
We can show that we like and welcome each other.
We can learn to accept each other.*

Read the page to the children and show the accompanying illustration. Ask questions like:

- "What do you think these children might be doing?"

33

- "What are they sharing?"
- "If one of these children tore another child's puppet, how do you think each of them would feel? What could they do about it?"
- "How do you take care of someone else's things?"
- "What if you're careful, but you still break something that someone trusted you not to break?"

ACTIVITY
Sharing Special Things

Materials needed:

- A belonging of your own to share with the group
- A broken toy
- A collection of stuffed animals, bean bag toys, or other special toys/items, one for each child (it's a good idea to have several duplicates of each toy, if possible)

Begin by telling the children that you have something special you want to share with them. Explain that the item belongs to you and that you're always very careful with it. Tell a little bit about why the item is so important to you.

Pass the item around the group. As the children take turns examining it, make positive statements reminding them to be careful, such as, "I know you'll treat it gently," and, "I trust you to be careful with it." If a child says, "Don't drop it!" or "Don't break it," you can say, "I know everyone will be very careful."

Next, show the children the broken toy. You might ask, "How do you think this toy got broken?" Talk about how the toy's owner and the person who broke it might feel. Discuss what each person could say or do about the accident. Present the idea that even when we're careful, we sometimes have an accident when using someone else's things.

Then show the children the collection of toys and invite them each to select one. Help them choose so they'll have something they like. Ask one or two volunteers why they chose the toy they selected. Ask the group, "If you share your toy with someone, how do you want that person to treat it?"

Tell the children that they may keep their toys for the day and/or share them, if they wish. Remind everyone to take care when using someone else's toy.

FOLLOW-UP

1. Discuss times when people take turns, such as waiting in line for the drinking fountain or waiting for a turn in a game. Point out that taking turns is a way of sharing.

2. Point out times when the children share things willingly and when they take care of each other's belongings: "Dante, I see you're letting Juana use your markers. I know Juana will remember to close the caps when she's done." "Danny's being very careful with Emma's book. I know Emma appreciates that."

3. Copy the Home Handout for this lesson, "10 Phrases That Help Children Share," to send home to the children's families. You might use the letter on page 4 to introduce the handout. Encourage the children to tell their families what they're learning about sharing and caring for other people's things.

LESSON NINE HOME HANDOUT

10 PHRASES THAT HELP CHILDREN SHARE

1. "May I see it?"

2. "I'll take care of it."

3. "I promise to do my best not to hurt it."

4. "I'll be careful with it."

5. "I'll watch over it."

6. "I'll put it where it won't get broken."

7. "You can leave it here until you want it."

8. "This is special to you."

9. "This is your favorite _____."

10. "We'll find a safe place to put it."

LESSON TEN

We Can Be Friends

> Accepting and being accepted by a friend is both affirming and fulfilling. As children learn what it means to be a friend, they gain important insights into the value of accepting and respecting others.

CONCEPT

Acceptance

GOALS

1. To teach children how to develop friendships.

2. To help children see that being a friend means accepting someone and being accepted in return.

DISCUSSING THE BOOK

(pages 20 and 21)

*I feel accepted when you invite me
to your home to play.
Or when you want to be my buddy
as we line up for playground time.
I feel accepted when you say I'm your friend.*

Read the page to the children and show the accompanying illustration. Ask questions like:

- "Do you think these children are friends? How can you tell?"

- "What do friends do together?"

- "How do people become friends?"

ACTIVITY 1
Matching Buddies

Materials needed:

- Buddy shapes cut from the pattern on page 38
- Crayons, pencils, and/or washable markers
- Large sheets of drawing paper
- White glue

Ahead of time, cut out the paired buddy shapes and cut the two shapes apart on the dotted line. Each child should have a single buddy shape.

Distribute the shapes. Tell the children to find a "buddy" with a shape that connects to their shape. (Show the children where the hands should connect.) If your group has an uneven number of children, take part in the activity as a buddy to one of the children.

Then have the partners work together to create a picture showing some things buddies do with each other. The children can color their characters, glue them to the drawing paper, and draw a picture around the shapes.

As the children color, notice how the partners are working together and what their pictures depict. You might say, "You seem to have lots of ideas about things buddies can do together."

Optional: You may want to copy and cut out an additional set of buddy shapes for each pair of children so they can make two pictures. Each child can then take a picture home.

ACTIVITY 2
Friends Around the Campfire

Materials needed:

- 3 or 4 flashlights
- Yellow and orange tissue paper
- Several sticks and small logs

Optional:

- Marshmallows and roasting sticks

This activity uses the melody and rhythm to "The Wheels on the Bus."

Turn the flashlights on. Drape tissue paper over the flashlights and arrange them with the logs to make a "campfire."

If you wish, turn out or dim the lights so it feels like nighttime. Gather the children in a circle around the fire. Talk about what people do around campfires: they might talk, roast marshmallows, tell stories, or sing songs. Then say, "We're going to sing around our campfire. Let's sing a song about being friends."

Talk briefly with the children about things that friends do together (play games, share toys, etc.). Then explain that the group can think up words to a song about being friends. Teach the song, using the children's ideas about what friends do together:

> When friends get together
> They *play a game,*
> *Play a game,*
> *Play a game.*
> When friends get together
> They *play a game.*
> That's what friends are for.

Lesson Ten

LESSON TEN HANDOUT: BUDDY SHAPES

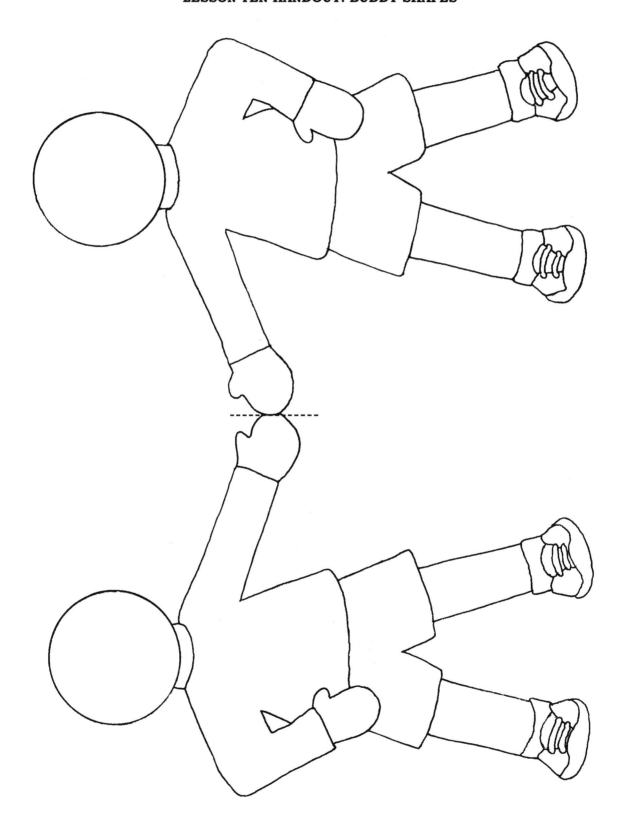

Invite the children to suggest other things that friends do together, then create and sing another verse to the song. The words don't need to rhyme; the meter doesn't need to be perfect, either. The goal is to have the children name and sing about a variety of different things friends do together, such as:

- share their toys
- sing a song
- laugh and play
- listen and care
- help each other
- say kind things.

The children might enjoy pantomiming the actions as they sing.

Optional: When you're finished singing, have the children "roast" marshmallows over the fire.

FOLLOW-UP

1. Discuss ways to make a new child or a visitor feel welcome.

2. When the children argue, take advantage of the teaching moment to remind them how friends need to treat each other. Teach the children some ways to resolve differences or defuse conflicts by asking before they take things, offering to help others, taking turns, and using words to work things out.

3. Have the children draw a picture of a time when someone made them feel welcome. Send the pictures home with the children. Encourage them to tell their families what they're learning about friendship.

4. Use the campfire at others times: Sing around it, talk around it, or have a snack around it. Let the children use the campfire in dramatic play.

Lesson Ten

LESSON ELEVEN

Tell Me Something About You

Listening without interrupting helps children learn to accept and value other people. Hearing about another person's experiences sparks children's interest and curiosity. Listening prompts children's own memories, while reinforcing and broadening their understanding of what people can have in common.

CONCEPT

Listening

GOALS

1. To build children's listening skills.
2. To help children value being listened to.
3. To help children understand what they can learn about themselves and others by listening.

DISCUSSING THE BOOK

(pages 22 and 23)

We can listen to each other.
This is a good way to get to know each other better.
We can learn more ways we're alike and different.

Read the page to the children and show the accompanying illustration. Ask questions like:

- "What are these children doing?"
- "Do you think they're listening to each other? Why do you think that?"

Your group might notice that the children in the illustration look interested and are paying attention to each other.

ACTIVITY 1
Ways to Listen

Materials needed:

- Chart paper and marker

Ask the children to think about a special memory they would like to share with the group. Invite a few volunteers to speak. Then ask:

- "Why do you like to tell other people about yourself?"
- "When you're speaking, what do you want the person who's listening to do?"
- "What are some ways to be a good listener?"

Use the Home Handout for this lesson ("5 Ways to Listen") as a guide for the activity. As the children present ideas, relate them to the ideas on the handout and write the listening skills on the chart paper.

At the end of the discussion, display the "Ways to Listen" list you've made.

ACTIVITY 2
Memory Banners

Materials needed:

- Roll of newsprint or craft paper, cut to 12" wide
- Scissors (for you)
- Crayons, colored pencils, and/or washable markers
- Wire hangers
- Stapler

Optional:

- Glitter, sequins, ribbon, and other decorative materials
- White glue

Ahead of time, cut strips of paper two to three feet long for the children.

Ask the children to recall a special memory. Explain that they can each make a "Memory Banner" illustrating that memory.

Give the children the banners and drawing materials. If they wish, they can decorate their banners with glitter or other materials.

Some children may find it difficult to recreate a memory on paper. Help them recall a part of a memory that's special to them. For example, one child might remember a pet dog; suggest that she draw a picture of the dog. Another child might remember green grass; suggest that he draw a design in green.

When the banners are done, fold the top (12") edge of each strip over a hanger and staple it in place. Invite volunteers to explain their banners to the group. Remind the children of the ways to listen (discussed in Activity 1) and carefully model the listening skills.

Display the children's banners by hanging them on the walls or from the ceiling.

FOLLOW-UP

1. Share your own memories with the children. Bring photographs, slides, or a video and tell about an experience you've had. Encourage the children to listen carefully and ask questions.

2. Keep the banners displayed and invite a few children each day to talk about their banners.

3. Have the children form pairs. Explain that the partners will practice speaking and listening. Start by having one partner speak while the other listens. Then invite some of the listeners to tell the large group what their partner said. Repeat, having partners switch roles.

4. Copy the Home Handout for this lesson, "5 Ways to Listen," to send home to the children's families. You might use the letter on page 4 to introduce the handout. Encourage the children to tell their families what they're learning about listening.

LESSON ELEVEN HOME HANDOUT

5 WAYS TO LISTEN

1. Look at the person who is speaking.

2. Listen carefully.

3. Don't interrupt.

4. Tell the person that you've heard.

5. Ask questions.

LESSON TWELVE

We Have Stories to Tell

> Stories—whether they're told, written, read, or shared in any other way—are a wonderful way to develop children's language and listening skills. As storytellers, children experience the power of sharing imaginative ideas and getting people's attention. As listeners, children can focus beyond themselves and share a listening experience.

CONCEPT

Listening

GOALS

1. To reinforce children's listening skills.

2. To provide an opportunity for children to share stories and to be heard.

3. To stimulate children's creativity through imaginative storymaking.

DISCUSSING THE BOOK

(pages 24 and 25)

*You listen when I tell you a story.
I listen to your stories, too.
I listen when you tell me about something important that happened to you.*

Read the page to the children and show the accompanying illustration. Ask questions like:

- "What do you think these children are doing?"

- "Does it look like they're having fun? Why do you think they're having fun?"

As part of your discussion, review the listening skills learned in Lesson Eleven (Activity 1, page 41).

Then turn the conversation to make-believe stories. You might say, "I wonder what story the child in the picture is telling. What might he be saying?"

Listen to a few suggestions from the children. If you wish, make up a story:

> I think the child is telling about an adventure he had with his cat. He spilled some grape juice and his cat stepped in it. The juice gave the cat special powers. If he leaped high enough, he could fly! The boy held onto his cat's back and together they flew high above the town. What do you think they saw?

Accept several responses. Then say:

- "What are some stories you've listened to or read in books?"
- "What is your favorite story from a book? Why do you especially like that story?"

After a few minutes, summarize by saying, "Books and pictures give us lots of ideas for stories. It's fun to tell stories. It's fun to listen to them, too."

ACTIVITY
Picture Stories

Materials needed:

- Poster or book of fine art prints*
- Writing and drawing paper
- Pencils, colored pencils, and/or washable markers

Optional:

- Cassette recorder and tapes

---

*Local art supply stores carry calendars and cards featuring artists' prints. Another good source for art prints are the Shorewood Visuals from the Dick Blick catalog. Three "First Discovery Art Books" for children are *Landscapes, Paintings,* and *Portraits,* all by Claude Delafosse and Gallimard Jeunesse. Museums are another excellent source for art prints, posters, and postcards. See "Recommended Readings and Resources," page 72.

Ahead of time, select a few art prints or pictures you feel will be meaningful to your group.

Show the pictures to the children, explaining that they're paintings or drawings made by *artists.* Invite the children to comment on the art: on colors, shapes, and the feelings the pictures evoke. As the children share their ideas, encourage the rest of the group to listen carefully and ask questions.

Tell the children that artists sometimes have a story in mind when they create their art. Invite the children to choose one of the pictures and draw or write a short story about what's happening in the picture. Encourage the children to both draw and write (assist those who need help writing). If you wish, offer the children the chance to tape-record their ideas.

Display the children's drawings and stories under the title "Pictures Tell Stories." If some children recorded stories, make the cassette player and tapes available for listening in the library area.

FOLLOW-UP

1. Over the next few days, ask volunteers to read or tell their stories about the art prints to the group, or invite them to retell the other children's stories.

2. Invite a storyteller from the community to share stories with your class. Prepare the children by reviewing the ways to listen discussed in Lesson Eleven (pages 40–42).

3. Encourage the children to share their stories with another class. Help the children practice their storytelling as needed.

4. Stimulate listening skills in a different way by having silent listening time. Have the children relax quietly and listen to the sounds around them. After a few minutes, ask the children to name the sounds they heard. If you like, list the sounds, along with simple pictures representing them, in a log and place it in the science area. Have the children listen at other times and draw or write about additional sounds in the log.

LESSON THIRTEEN

We Like Different Things

By making choices, children can experience their own uniqueness and recognize their similarities and differences. Children need many opportunities to choose. Besides fostering understanding and acceptance of themselves and others, learning to choose helps children develop skills to combat peer pressure. Some children may find it difficult to make a choice. Allow extra time for activities involving choosing, and support students who have difficulty.

CONCEPT

Understanding

GOALS

1. To provide opportunities for children to make choices.

2. To support children's decisions to do things in their own unique way.

3. To help children respect their own and other people's personal choices.

DISCUSSING THE BOOK

(pages 26 and 27)

We can tell each other about things we like and things we don't like.
We can try our best to understand each other.

Read the page to the children and show the accompanying illustration. Ask questions like:

- "What are the children in the picture doing?"

- "Who can tell me what this says?" (Point to the words "I like.") "What does that tell you about what the children are doing?"

45

- "What's different about what each child is doing?" (One is painting, one is holding a painting; they're depicting different things.)
- "What did they make? Why do you think they've each made something different?"
- "How do you think they decided what picture to make?"
- "Why do you think they like different things?"

Remind the children that everyone likes some different things. This is what makes each person unique.

ACTIVITY 1
Pattern Pictures

Materials needed:

- Drawing paper
- White glue
- Several different types of art materials such as yarn, Styrofoam peanuts, buttons, Popsicle sticks, and paper straws

Optional:

- A book showing patterns, such as *Kente Colors* by Debbi Chocolate and John Ward (see "Recommended Readings and Resources," page 72)

Ahead of time, make a simple pattern with one of the materials the children will use.

Introduce the activity by talking about patterns. Explain that a *pattern* is something that repeats. Draw several simple patterns as examples.

Tell the children that they can make pattern pictures. Show them the different art materials as well as the pattern you've made. Invite the children to describe the pattern. Then say, "You may choose some of these kinds of things to make any pattern you like. You can copy one of the ones we've seen, or make up a pattern of your own."

Help the children select materials and start their pattern pictures. If the children have trouble, suggest that they glue two items to their paper and then copy that pattern. Assist the children as needed.

Display the children's patterns and talk about how they're alike and different. Encourage comments about what the children like about the patterns. Ask the children to tell why they chose their material.

Tell the children, "Each of you made a pattern that's a little different from everyone else's." Talk about how the patterns are alike.

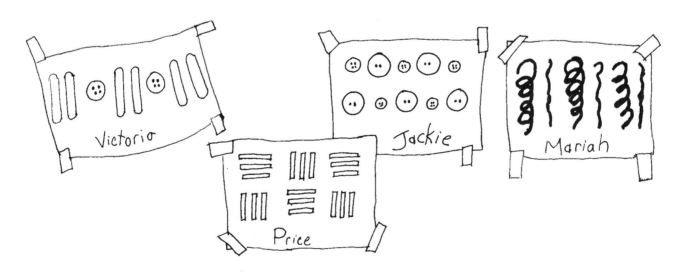

ACTIVITY 2
"Things We Like and Don't Like" Chart

Materials needed:

- Chart paper and marker
- Self-stick notes (3" square)
- Pencils or washable markers

Prepare a chart with three columns. Leave the top of the first column blank. Write "I Like" at the top of the second column and "I Don't Like" at the top of the third column.

Read or have a child read the words at the top of the chart. Tell the group that they can make a chart of things people in the group like and don't like. Ask for ideas, or name something yourself for starters. You might say, "I like reading the Sunday funny papers." Write "funny papers" under the top left line. Then ask, "Who else likes funny papers? Who doesn't like them?" Write your name on a self-stick note and place it under the "Like" column. Invite the children to write their names on notes and place them under one of the columns. Discuss why some people might like funnies and some might not.

Invite other children to tell something they like. Continue placing notes on the chart. As you add ideas, you may need to use additional sheets of chart paper. Reinforce the idea that some people like some things and others don't. We all like some different things. Tell the children, "What you like is up to you!"

When the activity is finished, post the chart(s) under the heading, "Things We Like and Don't Like." If the children wish, they can add other ideas and/or move their name stickers to different places.

FOLLOW-UP

1. Provide choices whenever possible. For example, at snacktime, offer the children crackers and cream cheese tinted with different food colors, or juice from a variety of colors of drinking cups. The children can choose which game to play outdoors or which story to read at storytime. Point out that each choice is different and that all choices are up to the person who makes them.

2. A "Yes and No Circle" is a simple activity that teaches choice-making. Have the group form a circle. While music plays, the children in the circle can clap their hands in time to it, while one person marches around outside the circle three times. When the music stops, the child says "I want to join the circle" or "I don't want to join the circle." The child then joins the circle or stands inside the circle. Play continues until everyone has had a chance to choose to join or not to join the circle.

3. Follow up Activity 2 by sharing some of the pattern ideas from *A Pair of Socks,* by Stuart J. Murphy and Lois Ehlert (see "Recommended Readings and Resources," page 72).

LESSON FOURTEEN

I Can Tell You What I'm Feeling

Children need to know that feelings are normal and natural to have, and that they can use words to describe how they feel. We can help children understand how to show and talk about feelings in ways that don't hurt others. As they talk about feelings and the words used to express them, children have a better understanding of common human experiences.

CONCEPT

Understanding

GOALS

1. To help children recognize different emotions.
2. To teach children words describing feelings.
3. To reinforce children's understanding that feelings are universal.
4. To encourage children to find positive ways to express and redirect strong feelings.

DISCUSSING THE BOOK

(pages 28 and 29)

I can tell you how I'm feeling.
You can tell me how you're feeling, too.
We can tell each other what we want
and what we need.
Sometimes we want the same things.
Sometimes we want different things.

Read the page to the children and show the accompanying illustration. Ask questions like:

- "Where are these children? What are they doing there?"

Point to each pictured child and ask:

- "How do you think *this* child is feeling?"
- "What do you think *this* child is saying or thinking?"

Encourage the children to suggest a variety of words describing feelings.

Summarize by telling the children that all people experience many feelings: sometimes they feel happy, sometimes sad, sometimes angry, sometimes excited, and sometimes scared. Feelings tell us about what's happening inside us.

ACTIVITY 1
Feeling Words Bulletin Board

Materials needed:

- Construction paper in a variety of colors, cut into 9" x 2" strips
- Marker
- Pushpins and bulletin board

With your group, brainstorm "feeling words." Write each of the words or phrases on a strip of paper. Invite the children to show how the feeling looks, using facial expressions and body language. Talk about how the feeling *feels*. You might say, "When I feel excited, my heart beats faster. I smile like this. I want to jump up and down!"

Brainstorm as many feeling words as possible. Talk about why people might have these different feelings, how the feelings look and feel, and some helpful ways to express them.

Here is a list of feeling words your group might compile:

- happy, silly, surprised, excited, joyful, eager
- sad, down, unhappy, tearful, gloomy, bored
- anxious, tense, fidgety, worried, nervous, impatient
- afraid, scared, frightened, terrified, fearful
- shy, unsure, bashful, left out, lonesome
- confused, embarrassed, guilty, ashamed
- angry, mad, upset, annoyed
- safe, calm, relaxed, hopeful

As you talk about feelings, ask the children, "Who can you talk to when you feel that way? What can you say?"

At the end of the activity, invite the children to help you pin the feeling words to the bulletin board. Have a supply of paper strips available for the children to add other feeling words.

Lesson Fourteen

ACTIVITY 2
Feelings Puppets

Materials needed:

- Clean white cotton tube socks, one sock per child
- Permanent fine-point markers in a variety of colors
- Buttons, beads, sequins, yarn, or ribbon for decorating the puppets
- Hot glue gun (for you)

Ahead of time, make a simple sock puppet so you'll have an example to share with the children.

Ask the children to name some feelings. For each feeling, ask: "How does that feeling look on someone's face? How does a person's body show that feeling?" Look at the "Feeling Words Bulletin Board" and invite volunteers to demonstrate how a face can show some of the different feelings. As you talk about feelings and how they look, show the children your sock puppet. Use the puppet to show some of the feelings you're discussing.

Tell the children that they can make feelings puppets out of socks. Give the children socks and markers and have them draw simple faces on their puppets. Encourage the children to use the puppets to show feelings by asking, "Can you make your puppet happy? Sad? Show me an excited puppet."

Then invite the children to choose some decorative items for adding details to their puppets. Use the hot glue gun to secure the decorations. Ask the children to write their names on the bottoms or inside edge of their puppets.

After the glue is completely dry, invite the children to show their puppets to the group and have people guess what the puppets are feeling. Remind the children that facial expressions and body language can mean many different things. That's why we also *talk about* feelings!

FOLLOW-UP

1. When the children have strong feelings, refer to the feeling words on the bulletin board and suggest positive ways to express feelings. You might say, "Lots of people seem to be looking forward to our field trip. Look at our feeling words. What are some words that tell how you're feeling?" Or, "Sasha, you seem upset with Kai. What words can you use to tell him how you feel?" Help the children express strong feelings in respectful, appropriate ways: "I'm angry that you used my puzzle without asking. Please ask first."

2. Follow up Activity 1 with music activities about feelings. A wonderful recording of feelings songs is Hap Palmer's *Getting to Know Myself* (see "Recommended Readings and Resources," page 72).

3. Follow up Activity 2 by having the children create simple skits or stories using the sock puppets. Make the puppets available in the dramatic play area.

4. Help the children write feeling words and draw a picture of something that shows those feelings. Send the pictures home with the children, and encourage them to tell their families what they're learning about showing and talking about feelings.

LESSON FIFTEEN

I Like to Be Understood

As teachers, we want to show empathy by understanding and being kind to children. Children need this empathy from us. They also need to learn to feel and show empathy to others. When the group talks about needs and feelings, children learn that everyone wants to feel understood. Learning to say "I'm sorry"—and mean it—is one way young children begin to empathize with others. Children also learn empathy as they look more closely at ways to tell others what they need and to ask for help. When someone is hurt or struggling, we can do what we can to make the situation better.

CONCEPT

Understanding

GOALS

1. To allow children a chance to reflect on the needs of others.
2. To introduce children to the idea of anticipating the needs of others.
3. To familiarize children with the words used to apologize.
4. To teach children ways to ask for help.

DISCUSSING THE BOOK

(pages 29 and 30)

We can try our best to be kind to each other.
Even when we don't agree with each other.
Even when we feel tired or upset.

Read the page to the children and show the accompanying illustration. Ask questions like:

- "What's happening in this picture?"
- "What do you think *this* child is feeling?" (Point to the child who has fallen.) "How can you tell?"
- "What is *this* child doing?" (Point to the other child.)
- "Have you ever fallen and gotten hurt? How did you feel? What did you do?"
- "Did anyone ever help you? How did it feel to be helped?"

Explain that we can understand how another person is feeling by watching and listening. We can show that we care and want to help.

ACTIVITY 1
"Care for Me" Role Plays

Tell the children: "I'm going to tell you a story. Please listen carefully and try hard to imagine how the people might be feeling." Tell this story:

> A group of children are eating lunch together. They're eating macaroni and cheese, corn, and peaches. They also have a carton of milk.

Stop and ask, "How do you think the children feel?" Then continue:

> While one child is opening his carton of milk, another child walks by and accidentally bumps him. The milk spills all over. The other children begin to laugh. One says, "Look! You have milk all over your lap!"

Ask questions like:

- "How do you think the child with the spilled milk feels?"
- "Are the other children being mean to him? Why do you think that?"
- "What can the child say and do to let the others know how he feels when they laugh at him?"
- "What can the other children do to show their friend that they care? How can they help him?"

Ask for volunteers to role-play the situation, showing the accident and the other children being kind and helpful.

Continue telling brief stories, discussing them, and asking volunteers to role-play them. Use situations your group of children will understand. Here are a few possible situations:

- A child has trouble zipping a jacket.
- A child is sad because she dropped her ice cream cone.
- A child is frustrated because he can't reach a game on a shelf.
- A child is upset because his toy is broken.

ACTIVITY 2
Talking About Being Sorry

Materials needed:

- Chart paper and marker

Remind the children of the story you told earlier in this lesson about the child whose milk was spilled at lunch. In the story, someone walked by and bumped the child. Ask the group, "What could the person who bumped the boy say to let him know it was an accident?"

Write the children's suggestions on the chart paper. Use the Home Handout for this lesson, "10 Ways to Say 'I'm Sorry,'" for some ideas.

Invite volunteers to tell the group about times they've done something they were sorry about. Ask questions like:

- "What did you say? What did you do?"

- "What else could you have said and done to show that you were sorry?"

- "How do you think the other person would feel then?"

- "When you apologize, what do you want the other person to say?" (Examples: "I know you didn't mean it." "That's okay." "I know you won't do it again.")

FOLLOW-UP

1. Talk about when people need help. Show the children pictures from magazines or books that illustrate parents helping children, doctors helping sick people, workers helping one another, and children helping others. Ask, "How can we tell when someone needs help? How can a person who needs help ask for it?"

2. Copy the Home Handout for this lesson, "10 Ways to Say 'I'm Sorry,'" to send home to the children's families. You might use the letter on page 4 to introduce the handout. Encourage the children to tell their families what they're learning about understanding people's feelings.

Lesson Fifteen

LESSON FIFTEEN HOME HANDOUT

10 WAYS TO SAY "I'M SORRY"

1. "I'm sorry."

2. "I didn't mean to do that."

3. "I feel bad that I said that."

4. "It was my fault."

5. "I apologize."

6. "I won't do that again."

7. "Please forgive me."

8. "I did something wrong."

9. "I wish I hadn't done that."

10. "I made a mistake."

From *A Leader's Guide to I'm Like You, You're Like Me,* by Cindy Gainer, copyright © 1998 Free Spirit Publishing Inc., Minneapolis, MN; 800/735-7323 *(www.freespirit.com).* This page may be photocopied for individual, classroom, or group work only.

LESSON SIXTEEN

I Can Be Kind

Talking about kindness follows naturally after learning about understanding and empathy. Children know that they like to be treated kindly. When playing with other children, they may have been teased, hit, or kicked, and they know these actions are hurtful. We can teach children words and actions that express kindness and help them recognize and use welcome touches. Of course, we can model these things as well. As we guide children to think and act kindly, we help them feel positive about themselves and others.

CONCEPT

Kindness

GOALS

1. To promote children's awareness of positive feelings, words, and actions.
2. To promote children's awareness that teasing and rough touches can hurt people.
3. To help children experience the pleasure that comes with being kind.

DISCUSSING THE BOOK

(pages 32 and 33)

*It's unkind to make fun of each other
or call each other names.
This is how feelings get hurt.
Let's be nice instead.*

Read the page to the children and show the accompanying illustration. Ask questions like:

- "What are the children in this picture doing?"
- "What do you think they might be saying to each other?"
- "Why do you think the children are having a good time?"
- "Who can tell me about a time when they had fun like this? Why was it fun?"

Help the children recognize that when people have fun together, they're being kind to each other and feeling good about themselves. Then ask:

- "What if someone started teasing, hitting, or throwing blocks?"
- "When someone teases you or calls you a name, how do you feel?"
- "When someone asks you to play and then plays nicely with you, how does that feel?"

Emphasize that kindness feels good for everyone. When one person is kind, other people may choose to be kind, too.

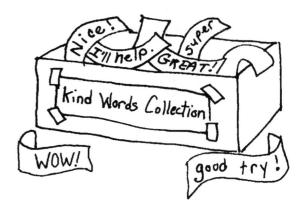

ACTIVITY 1
Kind Words Collection

Materials needed:

- Construction paper in a variety of colors, cut into 9" x 2" strips
- Marker
- Small box to hold the strips
- Tape or glue

Ahead of time, write the label and attach it to the box: "Kind Words Collection."

Ask the children to think of some words that might make them feel bad ("You're dumb," "You can't play with us," etc.). You might also ask the children, "Have you ever felt bad after saying something unkind to someone else? Why did you feel bad?"

Tell the group that they can start a collection of kind words. Invite volunteers to suggest words. If the children need help, use the Home Handout for this lesson, "30 Kind Things to Say," for some ideas. As the children make suggestions, write the words and phrases on the slips of paper.

After brainstorming, ask each of the children to draw a slip from the box. Have or help each child read the chosen slip and discuss the words, using questions like:

- "When could you say that?"
- "How would you feel if someone said that to you? Why would you feel that way?"

ACTIVITY 2
Good Touch Games

Materials needed:

- Book describing games that use simple touch ("Pat-a-Cake," "Peas Porridge Hot," "Miss Mary Mack," and "Ring Around the Rosie") such as *One Potato, Two Potato, Three Potato, Four: 165 Chants for Children,* compiled by Mary Lou Colgin (see "Recommended Readings and Resources," page 72)

Briefly review some of what your group has learned about being kind. Remind the children that it feels good both to be kind and to receive kindness.

Talk about kind touching, using words like the following:

> We can show kindness in the way we touch each other. Sometimes we feel like holding hands, or we want a hug. Sometimes we don't. Some kinds of touching don't feel good. Hitting or kicking or pinching hurts. It isn't kind to touch in ways that hurt.

NOTE: For a variety of reasons, some children aren't comfortable with physical contact. Be sensitive to children's needs in this area. If necessary, model ways to play the games without touching. This teaches kindness and respect as well, and allows children to enjoy the games in their own way.

Be aware that many parents believe that hitting and spanking are acceptable ways to discipline their children. Corporal punishment is legal in schools in many states. If a child says, "But Mommy hits me," you can acknowledge that some grown-ups who care for children do, in fact, hit their children. Then draw the children's attention back to the focus of this activity. You might say, "Some people may feel that hitting is okay, but it's not okay in our classroom." Or, "Hitting is not something that friends do to each other."

For information about reporting suspected abuse, see "What to Do If You Suspect That a Child Is Being Abused," page 59.

Then tell the children that they can play some games that use kind touching, such as clapping or holding hands. Tell the children, "If you don't want to be touched, tell your partner. You can play the game by clapping your own hands together instead."

FOLLOW-UP

1. At the beginning of each day, have the children draw a strip from the "Kind Words Collection" and find a way to use those words during an activity period. At the end of the period, invite a few volunteers to tell how someone was kind to them.

2. Consider adopting a class pet, such as a hamster. Have volunteers take the pet home over weekends. If you have a dog, cat, or another pet that is good with children, bring the animal to school and let the children handle and play with it. Caring for a pet is a wonderful way for children to learn about kind words and gentle touch.

3. Point out when the children treat each other kindly: "Jeremy, I think Maddie appreciated it when you helped her find her mittens." "Thank you for playing together so nicely." "I heard lots of kind words on the playground today."

4. Remind the children that sharing and taking turns are ways to show kindness. Encourage both during free time by having the children use a favorite classroom object for half the time and then trading with someone else. To help the children do this, set an egg timer and tell them they will exchange items when the timer rings.

5. Copy the Home Handout for this lesson, "30 Kind Things to Say," to send home to the children's families. You might use the letter on page 4 to introduce the handout. Encourage the children to tell their families what they're learning about kind words and actions.

LESSON SIXTEEN HOME HANDOUT

30 KIND THINGS TO SAY

1. "Great job!"
2. "Can I help you?"
3. "Thanks for your help!"
4. "I like it when you do that."
5. "It's nice to see you."
6. "Super!"
7. "I'm glad you're here."
8. "I like it!"
9. "Would you like to play?"
10. "Let's work together."
11. "You worked hard on that!"
12. "I appreciate your help."
13. "Fantastic!"
14. "You're a good friend."
15. "Please join us."
16. "I love you."
17. "We're a great team."
18. "I've missed you."
19. "Wow!"
20. "What do *you* think about it?"
21. "What would *you* like to do?"
22. "I'm proud of you."
23. "Everything will be okay."
24. "The kitty likes your soft petting."
25. "We have fun together."
26. "I can't wait to see you."
27. "Will you be my partner?"
28. "Can you show me how to do it?"
29. "I like to hear from you."
30. "You're special."

From *A Leader's Guide to I'm Like You, You're Like Me,* by Cindy Gainer, copyright © 1998 Free Spirit Publishing Inc., Minneapolis, MN; 800/735-7323 *(www.freespirit.com).* This page may be photocopied for individual, classroom, or group work only.

What to Do If You Suspect That a Child Is Being Abused

The regulations governing the reporting of child abuse differ from state to state. If you suspect that a child is being abused, contact your local social service or child welfare department. You can also obtain information about what to do and how to report child abuse from your local police department or district attorney's office.

If you're a teacher in a public school, consult with your school principal first to learn what the proper course of action is in your district.

Many states have specific guidelines identifying certain professionals as "mandatory reporters." This means that those professionals are required by law to report any suspected child abuse. Some states have provisions in their laws to protect the identity of those reporting child abuse. Check with your local agencies to determine your rights and responsibilities.

If a child reports abuse to you at any point during the course of "I'm Like You, You're Like Me," do not attempt to further interview the child. Let the child speak about what is happening to him or her, and affirm to the child how difficult it must be to be in that situation. After the lesson, and with regard to the laws of your state or organization, report the abuse promptly.

Do not ask the child leading questions about what is happening to him or her. Leave that to professionals who have been specially trained to deal with this sensitive issue.

Do not frighten the child by talking about reporting the abuse. In many cases, children who are being abused have been told by their abusers that very bad things will happen to them if they tell anyone. Report the situation immediately to the appropriate authorities and let them handle it.

For information on child abuse, contact:

The National Clearinghouse on Child Abuse and Neglect
330 C Street SW
Washington, DC 20447
Telephone: (703) 385-7565
Toll-free telephone: 1-800-394-3366
Web site: www.calib.com/nccanch

Prevent Child Abuse America
200 South Michigan Avenue, 17th Floor
Chicago, IL 60604
Telephone: (312) 663-3520
Web site: www.preventchildabuse.org

The National Exchange Club Foundation for the Prevention of Child Abuse
3050 West Central Avenue
Toledo, OH 43606-1700
Telephone: (419) 535-3232
Toll-free telephone: 1-800-924-2643
Web site: www.nationalexchangeclub.com/found.htm

LESSON SEVENTEEN

I Can Help

Everyone needs help at one time or another. Unintentionally, adults often underestimate children's ability to help. Being able to truly help someone else is essential to children's personal growth. Like sharing, taking turns, and speaking kindly, helping others gives children a positive sense of themselves and promotes feelings of goodwill.

CONCEPT

Kindness

GOALS

1. To help children recognize that everyone needs help.

2. To demonstrate that being helpful feels good.

3. To encourage children to think of ways they can help others.

DISCUSSING THE BOOK

(pages 34 and 35)

We're nice to each other when we hold hands.
When we say "Please" and "Thank you."
When we take turns.
When we give each other help.

Read the page to the children and show the accompanying illustration. Ask questions like:

- "What's happening in this picture?"

- "What is *this* child doing?" (Point to the child who is being helped.)

- "How do you think she feels? Why do you think that?"
- "What is *this* child doing?" (Point to the child who is tying the other child's shoes.)
- "How do you think he feels? Why do you think that?"
- "Who can tell about a time when someone helped you?"
- "Who can tell about a time when you helped someone else?"

Emphasize that helping someone is a kind thing to do. Let the children know how good it feels both to give and receive help.

ACTIVITY 1
"We Can Help" Picket Fence

Materials needed:

- Mural paper or a roll of newsprint
- Tape
- Permanent black marker (for you)
- Tempera paint (any single color) and brushes
- Crayons

Ahead of time, use the permanent black marker to draw a picket fence on the mural paper or newsprint. Leave room for some sky above the fence and some grass beneath it. Tape the paper to a wall in the classroom or hallway, or secure it to the floor.

Say to the children, "I have a fence that needs painting. I have some fresh paint. You can help me paint my fence."

Give the children time to paint individual pickets with a single color of paint. Children who finish more quickly than others can use crayons to draw grass, butterflies, insects, and other things around the fence.

Display the fence under the heading "We Can Help."

ACTIVITY 2
Talking About Helping

Ask the children to name some things that they can do to help others in the classroom. Some of the ideas the children might suggest include:

- putting away books and games
- feeding a classroom pet
- running an errand to another room

Lesson Seventeen

- helping someone read
- passing out art materials
- helping a friend zip a jacket
- cleaning up after snacktime
- giving someone a push on the swing.

As the children make suggestions, ask, "Who would that help? Why would someone like that kind of help?"

Continue discussing ways children can help at school, at home, and in the community.

FOLLOW-UP

1. Provide as many opportunities as you can for the children to help in the classroom. One way is by making a job chart and having the children sign up for different jobs. Include both words and simple pictures on your job chart, and use the chart to make sure all the children have a chance to help with things they're able to do. Some jobs might be:

   - acting as line leader
   - helping during lunch or snack
   - watering plants
   - collecting trash or recycling
   - feeding classroom pets
   - running errands in the building
   - passing out art materials
   - checking that things are put away in the art, library, social studies, dramatic play, and block areas.

2. Teach children words to use when asking for and giving help: "Please," "Thank you," "You're welcome," "May I?"

3. As a follow-up or variation to the fence-painting activity, create a different mural by drawing a house for children to illustrate with examples of helping.

4. Copy the Home Handout for this lesson, "20 Ways Children Can Help at Home," to send home to the children's families. You might use the letter on page 4 to introduce the handout. Encourage the children to tell their families what they're learning about helping others.

LESSON SEVENTEEN HOME HANDOUT

20 WAYS CHILDREN CAN HELP AT HOME

Children often enjoy helping out at home. You'll find that they're best able to help when they work alongside you or another family member. Some tasks aren't safe for children to do alone, so be sure to supervise. Even simple tasks are easier and more fun when you do them together. Keep in mind that children may not be able to carry out tasks completely, but show appreciation for a child's attempts to help in any way.

Here are just a few of the many things children can help you do at home:

1. Feed, walk, or groom a pet.
2. Set, clear, or wipe the table.
3. Pour cereal into bowls.
4. Toss a salad.
5. Mix ingredients for baking (and lick the spoon).
6. Wipe dishes or put them in the sink.
7. Run the vacuum cleaner.
8. Get the mail or newspaper.
9. Dust furniture.
10. Pick up toys and games.
11. Help put away groceries (a child-safe stool in the kitchen makes this safer and easier).
12. Help with outdoor chores like filling birdfeeders or pulling weeds.
13. Teach younger sisters and brothers simple games.
14. Read or look at books with brothers and sisters.
15. Sing a song to a baby.
16. Wrap gifts (using safety scissors).
17. Wash the car.
18. Sweep the patio, porch, walk, or driveway.
19. Sort clean socks or put away clothes.
20. Help plan family fun.

From *A Leader's Guide to I'm Like You, You're Like Me,* by Cindy Gainer, copyright © 1998 Free Spirit Publishing Inc., Minneapolis, MN; 800/735-7323 *(www.freespirit.com).* This page may be photocopied for individual, classroom, or group work only.

LESSON EIGHTEEN

I Can Be Patient

Children are learning to cooperate in many ways. One aspect of cooperation is patience. Many children (and grown-ups, too) find it hard to be patient with someone whose work style or skills are different from their own. To help children learn to be patient with each other, we can give them enjoyable projects with clear goals. We also need to guide them as they work, reinforcing their efforts and reminding them when they need to have a little more patience.

CONCEPT

Cooperation

GOALS

1. To provide opportunities for children to work together successfully.
2. To help children develop patience when working with others.

DISCUSSING THE BOOK

(pages 36 and 37)

Sometimes we work together to get things done.
We cooperate with each other.
We cooperate when we build
a sand castle together.
We cooperate when we play a game
all the way to the end, without fighting.

Read the page to the children and show the accompanying illustration. Ask questions like:

- "What are the children in this picture doing?"

- "Why do you think they're having a good time together?"
- "What are some things you and your friends do together?"
- "How do you make sure you get along with each other?"

The children's ideas might include sharing, not fighting, taking turns, and being kind and helpful.

Point out that when people work and play together, they need to be *patient*. To explain the concept, use words like the following:

> Being patient means waiting calmly. Sometimes a person might need a little extra time. Sometimes a person might want your help. If you're patient, the other person will have a chance to do his or her part. You'll both end up having more fun doing the project.

Then ask: "What do you think the people in the picture are doing to be patient?"

Activity 1
Puzzle Partners

Materials needed:

- Self-sealing plastic sandwich bags
- Permanent marker (for you)
- Piece of posterboard or tagboard for each child
- Crayons, colored pencils, and/or washable markers
- Safety scissors

Ahead of time, write each child's name in permanent marker on a plastic bag. Explain that the children can make puzzles. When they're done, they can put each other's puzzles together.

Have the children write their names on the back of the posterboard or tagboard. On the front, they can draw a picture. If the children need ideas for the picture, suggest they draw something they like to do with a friend. Tell the children that when they finish their drawings, they're going to cut them into pieces to make a puzzle.

As the children finish drawing, have them cut their picture into several pieces. Younger children may cut two or three pieces; older children may cut more. Encourage them to cut several large pieces instead of many tiny ones.

Give the children the bags with their names on them and have them put their puzzle pieces in the bag.

Then pair the children and have them trade puzzles. Say, "Each of you can put together the other person's puzzle. If one of you gets done first, wait patiently for your partner to finish. If you want help finishing, you may ask your partner."

As the children put the puzzles together, comment on the interesting puzzles and on how patiently and kindly the children are working together.

Lesson Eighteen

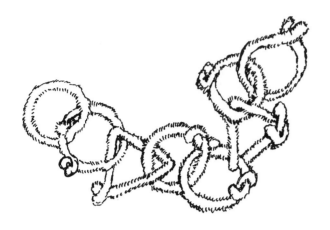

ACTIVITY 2
Links of Patience

Materials needed:

- Pipe cleaners or chenille stems in a variety of colors (have plenty for each pair of children)

Ahead of time, put together one or two simple patterns made of linked pipe cleaners. You might alternate colors or vary the shapes of the pipe cleaner links.

Show the children the sample links you've made. Tell them that they'll work together with a partner to make a simple pipe cleaner pattern. Demonstrate how to bend the pipe cleaners and twist them together to make the links.

Then pair the children and allow a short time for them to talk about their patterns. They may need to experiment a little to come up with a design. Then have them select the pipe cleaners they need and work together to link them into a pattern. To keep the activity short and simple, you might want to limit the number of links each pair can use.

Invite the children to show their patterns to the group. Ask for volunteers to describe some of the different patterns. Then link all the patterns together into a garland, and hang it from the ceiling or along the wall.

Say to the group: "Look what a beautiful garland you made by working patiently together."

FOLLOW-UP

1. Notice when the children cooperate and show patience: "I'm happy to see how patiently those of you who are dressed to go outside are waiting for those who are still getting ready."

2. Give the children other projects to do in pairs. Have them share a box of crayons to draw pictures. Or have them sort silverware by type or blocks by size, shape, or color.

LESSON NINETEEN

We Can Work Together

Cooperating can mean many things. Some projects children do together are relatively simple and enjoyable, while others are more complicated and difficult. Children need to understand that working together often requires people to persevere and think creatively. We can help children experience the benefits of a positive attitude in seeing a task through to completion.

CONCEPT

Cooperation

GOALS

1. To foster a positive, helpful attitude.

2. To help children see the benefits of persevering to finish a cooperative task.

3. To provide opportunities for children to work and play together cooperatively.

DISCUSSING THE BOOK

(pages 38 and 39)

When we cooperate, we can do almost anything!
We can play together and work together.
We can be friends.

Read the page to the children and show the accompanying illustration. Ask questions like:

- "What are the children in this picture doing?"

After the children respond, summarize by saying, "These children are working together in a garden. They're cooperating so they can all enjoy eating corn on the cob."

Continue discussing the book, asking questions like:

- "What would it be like if only one person were doing all the work in the garden?"
- "What would it be like if some of the children were grumbling or goofing off while they worked?"
- "Who can tell us about a time when you worked with a group of people to get a job done? What did you do? How did you work together?"
- "What if lots of people work on a job together, but the job is really hard? What if some people want to give up? Do you think they should keep working? Why?"
- "How do you think it feels when people work hard together and finish a job?"

Stress the importance of being willing to cooperate and keep working, even when something is hard to do.

ACTIVITY 1
Freight Train Fun

Materials needed:

- Chairs
- 3 or more large boxes
- Materials to fill the boxes (train cars), such as black checkers or dominoes for coal, blocks for lumber, red crepe paper for iron ore, or aluminum foil for silver

Optional:

- Flashlight
- Whistle

Prepare the children for this activity by talking about cooperating. You might say, "When we cooperate, we work together. Cooperating can be hard work."

Ask questions like:

- "What are some reasons it's important to cooperate?"
- "What can you do when it feels very hard to work together?"

Point out that people can accomplish many things when they cooperate. Sometimes they need to keep trying and think positively. Tell the children that they can practice these skills in an activity.

Have the children work together to create and load a freight train. Show them how to arrange the chairs and boxes to form a train with freight cars. Help them fill the cars with cargo. You might give one child a flashlight (to be the train's headlight) and another child a whistle (to be the train's whistle). Then have the children sit in the chairs and role-play while you tell a story like this:

> Here we go! We're leaving the station and the city. We're passing buildings and roads. Look how tall the buildings are. Now the buildings are getting smaller. We're going over a long bridge. We've moved so far from the city! Now we're in a desert. It's so hot we can feel the heat from the tracks! Look—there's a mountain up ahead. We have to

pull this heavy load up the mountain. It's hard! The mountain is very steep! Work hard. Keep pushing! Whew—we made it over the mountain! Now it's raining. We're getting wet! Let's keep the train moving fast to get through the rain.

Continue the story, emphasizing working hard and keeping a positive attitude. When the freight train arrives safely at its destination, the children can unload the cargo, put it away, and disassemble the train cars.

At the end of the activity, tell the children, "Some jobs are hard to do. When we cooperate and don't give up, we'll be glad in the end."

ACTIVITY 2
Block City

Materials needed:

- Blocks in a variety of shapes for constructing buildings
- People, vehicle, and animal figures

Optional:

- Polaroid camera
- Posterboard
- Marker

(If you have a large class, have the children work in groups of four or five. Set up separate areas or spread the activity over several days so everyone has a chance to participate.)

Have the block area or a large table or floor space available. Tell the children that they can work together to make a block city.

Help them decide how to build their city by asking questions like:

- "What buildings do you want to have in your city?"
- "Where will each building go?"
- "Who will build each one?"

Assist the children as needed while they work together. Remind them to be patient and help each other. Notice and remark on how the group is cooperating.

Optional: Take a picture of the children's structures and display the pictures on a poster entitled "Look What We Can Build Together!"

FOLLOW-UP

1. As a follow-up to Activity 1, read *The Little Engine That Could* by Watty Piper and sing, listen, and move to train songs such as "Little Red Caboose" (see "Recommended Readings and Resources," page 72).

2. Leave the block cities up for several days so that the children can play with them.

3. Brainstorm ways to cooperate. Your list might include:

   - building a sand castle with a friend
   - playing a board game with another child
   - cleaning a room with a group of children
   - building a snowman outdoors
   - decorating the classroom for a special day.

Lesson Nineteen

LESSON TWENTY
We Can Cooperate and Have Fun Together

Repeating, reinforcing, and synthesizing concepts to make them truly meaningful to children is important. A creative group project provides a review of ideas as well as a concrete way for children to experience the satisfaction and enjoyment that people working together can achieve.

CONCEPT

Putting It All Together

GOALS

1. To reinforce children's understanding of things they have learned about similarities and differences, acceptance, listening, understanding, being kind, and cooperating.

2. To provide a creative, cooperative project for children.

DISCUSSING THE BOOK

(pages 40 and 41)

I'm like you, you're like me.
But we're not exactly the same.
That's why I like you
and you like me.

Read the page to the children and show the accompanying illustration. Ask questions like:

- "What are the children in this picture doing?"

- "Why do you think the children are having a good time together?"

Address the concepts the children have explored throughout the "I'm Like You, You're Like Me" lessons. Ask questions like:

- "What might be some ways the children are alike?"
- "What might be some ways they're different from each other?"
- "Do you think the children enjoy being with each other? Why?"
- "What are some ways these children might take turns and share?"
- "How do you think the children help each other?"
- "How are these children cooperating with each other?"

ACTIVITY
Weaving Ideas
Materials needed:

- Sheets of posterboard in a variety of colors, several sheets of each color
- Marker
- Scissors or paper cutter (for you)
- Plastic six-pack rings from soda cans
- Sheets of 9" x 12" construction paper
- Stapler

Cut strips of posterboard approximately 9" x 1", enough so you and each child will have several strips of each color. Weave a strip of each color through a six-pack ring, as shown.

Tell the children they can each make a weaving for a colorful bulletin board. Show them the weaving you've made and demonstrate how to weave the strips through the six-pack rings.

Then distribute strips and six-pack rings and have the children create weavings. Assist those who need it. Allow the children to weave in whatever way they like.

Give the children a blank sheet of construction paper and have them write their name on one side. On the other side, help them staple their weavings to the construction paper.

Invite the children to show their finished weavings to the group. Discuss the ways that individual children's weavings are alike and different.

Display the weavings in a single colorful pattern on the bulletin board with the label "I'm Like You, You're Like Me." Point out to the children that they all worked together to create the large, colorful weaving.

FOLLOW-UP

Read the children's book *I'm Like You, You're Like Me* to the group from start to finish. As they listen and discuss the book, the children can recall many of the things they talked about and worked on together.

Recommended Readings and Resources

Blizzard, Gladys S. Come Look with Me: Enjoying Art with Children (Charlottesville, VA: Thomasson-Grant, 1993). Full-color art reproductions along with artist biographies and questions that encourage children to look, think, and talk about each piece of art.

Chocolate, Debbi, illustrations by John Ward. Kente Colors (New York: Walker & Co., 1996). This children's book is loaded with beautiful, full-color illustrations of West African Kente cloth.

Colgin, Mary Lou, comp. One Potato, Two Potato, Three Potato, Four: 165 Chants for Children (Beltsville, MD: Gryphon House, 1982). A selection of fingerplays, chants, and nursery rhymes, including "Pat-a-Cake" and "Miss Mary Mack."

Delafosse, Claude, and Gallimard Jeunesse. Landscapes, Paintings, and Portraits (New York: Scholastic, 1993). Three "First Discovery Art Books" introduce children to classic works of fine art.

Dick Blick Catalog. An excellent source of art materials, including fine art prints from Shorewood Visuals. Write to Dick Blick Catalog, P.O. Box 1267, 695 Route 150, Galesburg, IL 61402-1267. Toll-free telephone: 1-800-828-4548. Web site: www.dickblick.com

Gibbons, Gail. Happy Birthday! (New York: Holiday House, 1986). This children's book explores historical traditions, beliefs, and celebrations tied to birthdays.

Lionni, Leo. Swimmy (New York: Pantheon, 1968). In this story about the value of being different, Swimmy helps a school of fish protect themselves by swimming together as if they're one large fish. Because he's a different color, Swimmy is able to help the school of fish protect themselves.

Metropolitan Museum of Art. An excellent source for art prints, posters, and postcards. Write to Metropolitan Museum of Art, Special Services Office, Middle Village, NY 11381-0001. Toll-free telephone: 1-800-468-7386. Web site: www.moma.org

Morris, Ann, photographs by Ken Heyman. Houses and Homes (New York: Lothrop, Lee & Shepard, 1992). Describes and illustrates a variety of houses from around the world and discusses what makes them homes.

Murphy, Stuart J., illustrations by Lois Ehlert. A Pair of Socks (New York: HarperCollins Children's Books, 1996). A "MathStart Book" that uses socks to teach children about patterns.

National Gallery of Art. Another source of art prints, posters, and postcards. Write to National Gallery of Art, Mail Orders, 2000-B South Club Drive, Landover, MD 20785. Toll-free telephone: 1-800-697-9350. Web site: www.nga.gov

Palmer, Hap. Getting to Know Myself. A wonderful album of children's songs about feelings. Write to Educational Activities Inc., P.O. Box 392, Freeport, NY 11520. Toll-free telephone: 1-800-645-3739.

Piper, Watty. The Little Engine That Could (New York: G.P. Putnam & Sons, 1986). With the help of her cargo-load of toys, a little engine is able to pull the train over a mountain.

Teaching Tolerance. A free biannual magazine filled with stories and ideas about how children and educators are working to respect and value differences. Write to the Southern Poverty Law Center, 400 Washington Avenue, Montgomery, AL 36104. Telephone: (334) 956-8200. Web site: www.splcenter.org

Wee Sing Fun and Folk (New York: G.P. Putnam & Sons, 1995). A good source for train songs such as "Little Red Caboose" and "Train Is A'Comin'."

About the Author/Illustrator

Cindy Gainer has a B.F.A. with Early Childhood and Art Education Certification from Seton Hill College in Greensburg, Pennsylvania, and she is currently participating in the Gestalt Training for Professionals Program in Pittsburgh. She is the coauthor and illustrator of the award-winning books *Good Earth Art: Environmental Art for Kids* (Bright Ring Publishing) and *MathArts: Exploring Math through Art for 3 to 6 Year Olds* (Gryphon House). She has taught art to children from grades kindergarten through 12 in Pennsylvania schools, appeared on television, and has given numerous workshops to teachers and students as an author/illustrator. Cindy owns Little Red Schoolhouse, a preschool for four- and five-year-olds, where she is actively involved in teaching young learners and fostering positive child development. Cindy resides in Jeannette, Pennsylvania, with her husband, Bill Matrisch, and their son, August.

Other Great Books from Free Spirit

Just Because I Am
A Child's Book of Affirmation
by Lauren Murphy Payne, M.S.W., illustrated by Claudia Rohling, M.S.W.
Warm, simple words and enchanting full-color illustrations strengthen and support children's self-esteem. Ideal for early elementary, preschool, day care, and the home. For ages 3–8.
$8.95; 32 pp.; softcover; color illus.; 7⅝" x 9¼"

A Leader's Guide to Just Because I Am
A Child's Book of Affirmation
by Lauren Murphy Payne, M.S.W., and Claudia Rohling, M.S.W.
Thirteen lessons reinforce the message of the child's book. Includes activities, questions, and reproducible Home Handout masters. For preschool through grade 3.
$13.95; 56 pp.; softcover; illus., 8½" x 11"

We Can Get Along
A Child's Book of Choices
by Lauren Murphy Payne, M.S.W., illustrated by Claudia Rohling, M.S.W.
Simple words and inviting illustrations teach children how to get along with others and resolve conflicts peacefully. For ages 3–8.
$9.95; 36 pp.; softcover; color illus.; 7⅝" x 9¼"

A Leader's Guide to We Can Get Along
A Child's Book of Choices
by Lauren Murphy Payne, M.S.W., and Claudia Rohling, M.S.W.
Fifteen lessons reinforce the messages of the child's book. Includes activities, questions, and reproducible Home Handouts for parents. For preschool through grade 3.
$14.95; 64 pp.; softcover; illus., 8½" x 11"

I Like Being Me
Poems for Children About Feeling Special, Appreciating Others, and Getting Along
by Judy Lalli, M.S., photographs by Douglas L. Mason-Fry
Rhyming poems and black and white photographs explore issue important to young children—being kind, solving problems, and more. For ages 3–8.
$9.95; 64 pp.; softcover; B&W photos; 8¼" x 7¼"

To place an order or to request a free catalog of Self-Help for Kids® *and* Self-Help for Teens® *materials, please write, call, email, or visit our Web site:*

Free Spirit Publishing Inc.
217 Fifth Avenue North • Suite 200 • Minneapolis, MN 55401-1299
toll-free 800.735.7323 • local 612.338.2068 • fax 612.337.5050
help4kids@freespirit.com • www.freespirit.com